Just Being
Audrey

By
Margaret Cardillo

Illustrated by
Julia Denos

BALZER + BRAY
An Imprint of HarperCollinsPublishers

To my mother, who is very Audrey
—M.C.

For Audrey and for the children
she loved around the world
—J.D.

Balzer + Bray is an imprint of HarperCollins Publishers.

Just Being Audrey
Text copyright © 2011 by Margaret Cardillo
Illustrations copyright © 2011 by Julia Denos
All rights reserved. Printed in the U.S.A.
No part of this book may be used or reproduced in any manner whatsoever without written
permission except in the case of brief quotations embodied in critical articles and reviews.
For information address HarperCollins Children's Books, a division of HarperCollins Publishers,
10 East 53rd Street, New York, NY 10022.
www.harpercollinschildrens.com

Library of Congress Cataloging-in-Publication Data
Cardillo, Margaret.
 Just being Audrey / by Margaret Cardillo ; illustrated by Julia Denos.—1st ed.
   p. cm.
 ISBN 978-0-06-185283-1 (trade bdg.)—ISBN 978-0-06-185284-8 (lib. bdg.)
  1. Hepburn, Audrey, 1929–1993. 2. Motion picture actors and actresses—United States—
Biography. I. Denos, Julia, ill. II. Title.
PN2287.H43C37 2011   2010003982
791.4302'8092—dc22   CIP
[B]   AC

Typography by Jennifer Rozbruch
11 12 13   LPR   10 9 8 7 6 5 4 3
❖
First Edition

"I never think about myself as an icon . . .
I just do my thing."
—Audrey Hepburn

More than anything, Audrey wanted to be a ballerina. She was too tall, her feet were too big, and her neck was too long. Still, Audrey danced on. She held fairy-tale ballets in her yard, the trees and squirrels her audience.

Audrey's brothers would tease her, always off in her own world. But her mother understood. "It is just like Audrey to do her own thing."

Audrey struggled with *en pointe*—dancing on her toes—
but she loved a challenge. So she practiced more than all the
other ballerinas in class. Some of the girls laughed at Audrey,
saying her teeth were crooked and her eyes seemed too big
for her head. Audrey knew she looked different, but it didn't
matter much to her.

She wanted only one thing: to be the prima ballerina of all of Europe.

Her mother reminded her that there were more important things than fame. "Others matter more than you, dear," she said. "You must always be kind."

When Audrey was ten years old, World War II broke out in Europe. Her family fled to Holland, but the Nazi troops marched into the country and right up to the Hepburns' front door. Although her mother was a baroness, Audrey's childhood was turning out to be anything but noble.

Her family, and forty other people, hid in a small house in the country. There was no heat and little food. Supplies were quickly running out, and people were starting to feel desperate.

Despite everything, Audrey continued to dance. She took the children into the dining room to practice ballet routines. The dancers held performances to raise money for Resistance troops. The audience could not clap, for fear of being found, but the smiles on their faces told Audrey all she needed to know.

One day there was a knock on the front door, and everyone froze. Had they been discovered? But after years of bad news, there was finally something to celebrate. The war had ended, and volunteers from the United Nations had arrived, bringing food, clothing, and medicine.

One volunteer gave Audrey a chocolate bar. She ate it so quickly she got a stomachache. But it was the most delicious thing she had ever tasted. Audrey never forgot that kind gesture.

After the war ended, Audrey
and her mother moved to London.
They had very little money. In fact, Audrey had
only a few blouses and skirts and one colorful scarf.
But she could tie the scarf twenty different ways to
make a new outfit every day.

Audrey soon realized that her dream of being a ballerina
was not going to become a reality. She was simply too tall,
and no amount of practice could change that. She decided
to try acting instead.

She landed a few small roles; one took her to the south of France. Colette, the famous French writer, spotted Audrey. Colette needed an actress for the lead role in her play *Gigi* that was opening on Broadway in New York City.

"*C'est Gigi!* It is my Gigi!" Colette announced.

Surely Colette was mistaken. Audrey had no acting experience.

"She has that *je ne sais quoi* . . . that certain something!"

With that, Audrey was on her way to Broadway.

New York was very different from the countryside.
But Audrey rehearsed so much, she hardly noticed.
To make up for her inexperience, she worked harder
than anyone else.

While Audrey was performing on Broadway, the movie director William Wyler was looking for a fresh face for his new Hollywood film. When he saw Audrey, he knew he'd found it.

In the movie *Roman Holiday*, Audrey plays Princess Ann, who falls in love with a journalist. By the time the movie came out, *everyone* had fallen in love with Audrey. She even won an Oscar for her performance.

Audrey went on to star in some of Hollywood's biggest movies, including *Funny Face*, *Sabrina*, and *My Fair Lady*. From a party girl in *Breakfast at Tiffany's* to a nun in *The Nun's Story*, Audrey took roles that challenged her and she made them her own.

Audrey often played characters who went through some kind of transformation, both inside and out. But in real life, Audrey always knew just who she was, and just where she had come from.

Audrey had become more than an actress; she was an inspiration. While most Hollywood starlets were curvy and wore glamorous outfits, Audrey would only be herself. She was always slender, she wore her hair short, and her clothes were simple and elegant. It was such a different style that it got its own name: the Audrey look.

And the very things that made her appear awkward as a child? They were precisely the things that made her beautiful as an adult. From Los Angeles to New York, Paris to Tokyo, there were imitations of her walking about town. Everyone wanted to be just like Audrey.

She didn't behave like most movie stars, either. She was always on time and studied her lines to perfection. After filming, Audrey would cook warm spaghetti dinners for the cast and crew. She was the kindest actress any of them had ever worked with.

Audrey starred in more than two dozen movies, but her dream role was being a mother. She spent her days with her sons, Sean and Luca, and tended her garden in the afternoons. She had never been happier.

Once her children had grown, she decided to put her fame to good use. In 1988, Audrey became a Goodwill Ambassador for an organization called UNICEF. It was the very same organization that had helped her as a child during the war.

Audrey traveled all over the world bringing aid to children in need. "Like with flowers," she said, "it's the same with children: With a little help they can survive and they can stand up and live another day."

Her finest performance came in 1989. Audrey spoke to Congress to ask for help for all of the children she had met during her travels. "I am here today to speak for children who cannot speak for themselves," she said. "Every child has the right to health, to tenderness, to life."

Her words were so moving and eloquent that people listened. Funding for UNICEF doubled, and she inspired fellow actors to join the movement.

For her efforts, Audrey was awarded the Presidential Medal of Freedom in 1992, one of the highest honors a person can receive.

Audrey's life was not always a fairy tale, but she chose hope over sorrow. Her legacy remains; it is in the loveliness of her movies, in the kindness she showed others, and on the faces of the children she helped around the world.

And, if you look closely, you can still see
the Audrey look about town.

Author's Note

I was first introduced to Audrey Hepburn in middle school, while deciding who to be for my class Character Parade. In an attempt to inspire me, my mother popped *Roman Holiday* into the VCR. As soon as the credits rolled, I was demanding an encore. *Breakfast at Tiffany's*, *My Fair Lady*, *Sabrina*—the day turned into an Audrey marathon. I was enthralled, not just by Audrey's beauty, but by her spirit and joie de vivre. She could get out of any jam with a winning smile and a witty comment. As a little troublemaker myself, I could see a bit of myself in her.

Like many of her fans, I was first drawn to Audrey for her movies. However, my research for this book uncovered that her life outside pictures was much more intriguing than her life inside them. And at a time when so many actresses are popular for the wrong reasons, I wanted to celebrate a woman who used her celebrity for the right ones.

Years have passed since the Character Parade and my first brush with Audrey Hepburn—and still today, I want to be like her. Audrey taught me what every girl needs to learn: the importance of being myself. In her own words, Audrey taught me to just do my own thing.

Illustrator's Note

Before starting this project, there was much I did not know about Audrey Hepburn. Yes, I wore echoes of her fashion trends every day—walking around wearing ballet flats, scarves tied in bows, and "skinny" jeans—but knowing Audrey is about more than merely emulating her style.

So when Margaret Cardillo's manuscript about this extraordinary woman came to me, I had to start from the beginning. I pored over Audrey's films, read her biographies, studied her costumes, heard her interviews, walked into her life, and consequently fell in love! There are so many facets of Audrey to admire: the little girl enduring World War II; the young woman glowing in Givenchy creations; the wise woman on a dusty Ethiopian plain cradling the frail children she adored.

I am aware that I fall into line behind millions of lifelong and adoring fans, but maybe I am luckier for being late to the game. I was able to meet Audrey in my own world, on my own time, in the quiet of blank white drawing paper. Audrey's world was paradise for me to paint: My reference material included rich Technicolor films, vintage family photographs, couture collections, and classic silhouettes.

During months of studying how those smart cotton blouses tucked perfectly into her pedal pushers and how her de Rossi eyebrows sat just below her bangs, I befriended the soul behind the style. Audrey left me with this inspiration: to simply remain in love with life, to be openhearted. I'm honored to have painted a life like hers.

Timeline

May 4, 1929   Audrey Hepburn is born in Brussels, Belgium.

May 10, 1940   Germany invades Holland, where Audrey is living.

May 4, 1945   Holland is liberated from Nazi control, and Audrey turns sixteen.

1948   Stars in her first film, *Dutch in Seven Lessons*.

1951   The writer Colette spots Audrey in France and asks her to play the role of Gigi on Broadway.

September 2, 1953   Opening of Audrey's first Hollywood film, *Roman Holiday*, with Gregory Peck.

1954   Becomes one of only three actresses to win an Oscar (for *Roman Holiday*) and a Tony (for *Ondine*) in the same year.

1954   Audrey meets renowned fashion designer Hubert de Givenchy while filming *Sabrina*.

September 25, 1954   Marries actor Mel Ferrer (divorced 1968).

July 17, 1960   Audrey's first son, Sean, is born.

1961   Audrey stars as Holly Golightly in *Breakfast at Tiffany's*.

January 18, 1969   Marries Dr. Andrea Dotti in Rome, Italy (divorced 1982).

February 8, 1970   Audrey's second son, Luca, is born.

1980   Meets Robert Wolders at a dinner party. He will be her companion until her death.

1988   Becomes a UNICEF International Goodwill Ambassador.

April 6, 1989   Speaks to Congress about her experiences.

December 11, 1992   Awarded the Presidential Medal of Freedom.

January 20, 1993   Audrey passes away in her home in Tolochenaz, Switzerland.

1993   Becomes one of only five people to win an Oscar, a Golden Globe, a Tony, a Grammy, and an Emmy.

Bibliography

Selected Books

Diamond, Jessica Z., and Ellen Erwin. *The Audrey Hepburn Treasures: Pictures and Mementos from a Life of Style and Purpose*. New York: Atria Books, 2006.

Ferrer, Sean Hepburn. *Audrey Hepburn, An Elegant Spirit*. New York: Atria Books, 2003.

Harris, Warren G. *Audrey Hepburn: A Biography*. New York: Simon & Schuster, 1994.

Hellstern, Melissa. *How to Be Lovely: The Audrey Hepburn Way of Life*. New York: Dutton, 2004.

Higham, Charles. *Audrey: The Life of Audrey Hepburn*. New York: Macmillan, 1984.

Keogh, Pamela. *What Would Audrey Do?* New York: Gotham Books, 2008.

Spoto, Donald. *Enchantment: The Life of Audrey Hepburn*. New York: Three Rivers Press, 2006.

Improving the Health of the Poor, a Development Cornerstone: Hearing Before the International Task Force of the Select Committee on Hunger, House of Representatives, One Hundred First Congress, First Session, Held in Washington, D.C., April 6, 1989. Washington: Government Printing Office, 1989.

Other Selected Resources

Audrey Hepburn's Official Website: www.audreyhepburn.com

Gardens of the World with Audrey Hepburn (Part Two). Directed by Bruce Franchini. Perennial Productions and Public Broadcasting Service (PBS), January 21, 1993.